# Lineman, The Unsung Hero

## Written by Michelle Larson

## Illustrated by Susan Shorter

*AuthorHouse™*
*1663 Liberty Drive*
*Bloomington, IN 47403*
*www.authorhouse.com*
*Phone: 1-800-839-8640*

*Published by AuthorHouse 4/12/2012*

*ISBN: 978-1-4685-6662-8 (sc)*

*Library of Congress Control Number: 2012905356*

*Any people depicted in stock imagery provided by Thinkstock are models,*
*and such images are being used for illustrative purposes only.*
*Certain stock imagery © Thinkstock.*

*This book is printed on acid-free paper.*

*Because of the dynamic nature of the Internet, any web addresses or links contained in this book may have changed*
*since publication and may no longer be valid. The views expressed in this work are solely those of the author and do not*
*necessarily reflect the views of the publisher, and the publisher hereby disclaims any responsibility for them.*

## Lineman, The Unsung Hero

If your power goes out,

don't act like a baby and scream and shout.

Just remember:

if it was your daddy working on a high-voltage line,

you would want him to be safe and take his time.


*For Matt, Maddie, and Carter*

Many people take electricity for granted.

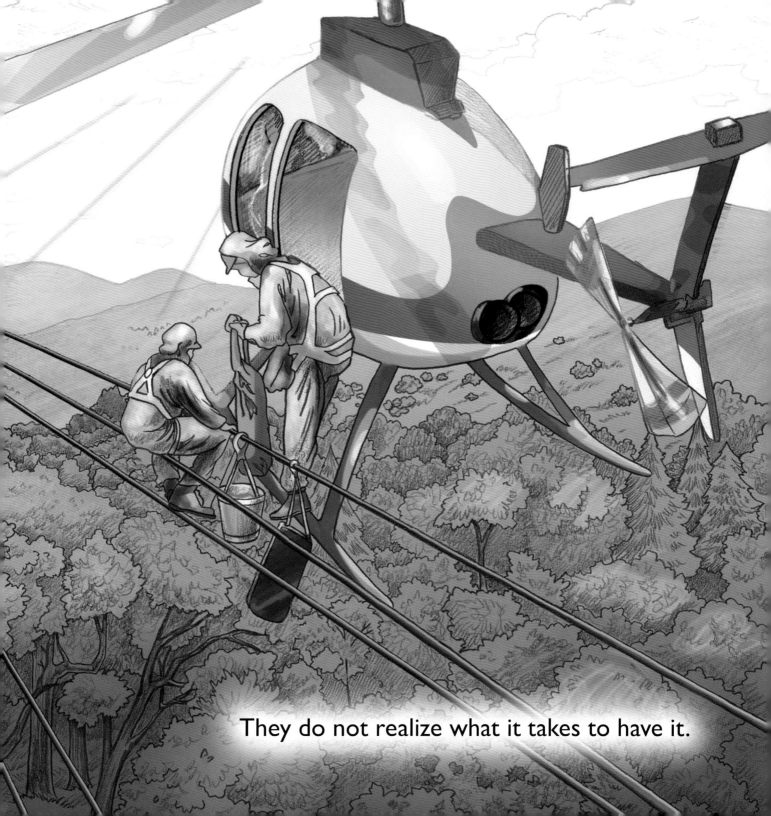

They do not realize what it takes to have it.

Linemen constantly work hard to keep us in power.
They can get called out at any hour.

They work with high voltages every day.
Safety comes first in every way.

Linemen have to be ready for accidents and disasters.
They keep emergency crews safe from electrical hazards.

They depend a lot on one another
and care for each other just like a brother.

Linemen work straight through the hottest and coldest days.

They rarely take a break..... or so they say!

Linemen get to operate a big bucket truck,

but don't worry..... they hardly ever get stuck!

Linemen use a "shot gun" every day,
but not in the hunting way.

Their work calls for a set of hooks,
a strapping body, and very good looks!

From hanging a "pot" to working it "hot," being a lineman requires a lot!

Linemen are strong, proud, and brave because that's what it takes to make it in this trade.

They seldom get the recognition that is due,
yet they continue to work hard for me and you.

So, the next time you turn on a light,
think of a lineman and all of his might.
And when you see him hanging proudly from his hooks,
or strapped into a bucket up in the sky,
don't hesitate to shout "Thanks!" and wave hi!

*God Bless and Protect*

*Our Linemen*